D0232915

PRAYERS & PROMISES

for

Couples

BroadStreet
PUBLISHING

CONTENTS

Introduction

Spending quality time together as a couple can be difficult, but it's incredibly important for maintaining a healthy relationship! One of the best ways to strengthen your relationship is to spend time together with God.

Prayers & Promises for Couples incorporates more than 70 themes to help you receive inspiration found in the promises of God's Word. Uplifting prayers offer the opportunity for deeper reflection.

By staying connected to God, and believing the promises of his Word, you can live a fulfilling, blessed life in close relationship with each other and with your heavenly Father.

Acceptance

"The Father gives me the people who are mine.
Every one of them will come to me,
and I will always accept them."

JOHN 6:37 NCV

The LORD does not see as man sees; for man looks at the
outward appearance, but the LORD looks at the heart.

1 SAMUEL 16:7 NKJV

If God is for us, who can be against us?

ROMANS 8:31 ESV

Before he made the world, God chose us to be his very
own through what Christ would do for us; he decided
then to make us holy in his eyes, without a single fault—
we who stand before him covered with his love.

EPHESIANS 1:4 TLB

God, what a wonder that you see us in ways that no one else does. Not only did you choose us before the beginning of time as your own, but nothing can change your mind about us! Thank you for accepting us as we are, not as how we should be. Help us to accept ourselves and each other as you do. We know we don't have to do anything to earn your love. As we learn to receive your love without condition, help us to love each other the way you do.

How does God's acceptance of you help you to be more accepting of each other?

Affection

I am my beloved's,
And his desire is toward me.

SONG OF SOLOMON 7:10 NKJV

You make known to me the path of life;
you will fill me with joy in your presence,
with eternal pleasures at your right hand.

PSALM 16:11 NIV

My beloved speaks and says to me:
"Arise, my love, my beautiful one,
and come away,
for behold, the winter is past;
the rain is over and gone.
The flowers appear on the earth,
the time of singing has come."

SONG OF SOLOMON 2:10-12 ESV

Father, please help us cancel out the lies of the enemy which tell us we are unlovable or need to be somebody we're not. Your affection is hard to fathom because we struggle to see past our own depravity. Your love, however, is not conditional of our deservedness but is an overflow of your goodness. Thank you for creating us to be the recipients of your affection. Help us to be catalysts of your affection to each other.

How do you feel the affection of God in your life?

Anxiety

You will keep in perfect peace
those whose minds are steadfast,
because they trust in you.

ISAIAH 26:3 NIV

"Don't let your hearts be troubled.
Trust in God, and trust also in me."

JOHN 14:1 NLT

Give all your worries to him,
because he cares about you.

1 PETER 5:7 NCV

I call out to the LORD when I'm in trouble,
and he answers me.

PSALM 120:1 NIRV

Lord, you know our hearts and our every thought. You know when we sit and when we stand. You know our history and our future. There are no mysteries to you. When doubts and fears threaten to overwhelm us, be the peace that calms the storm. We will remember together who you are: our defender, Savior, and Good Shepherd. You are our hope. We will trust in you even when it takes everything inside of us to choose it. When we cannot see the way out, we know that you see it all so clearly and you are never overwhelmed. We trust you, God.

What steps can you take to be less anxious and more trusting?

Assurance

To him who is able to do immeasurably more than all we
ask or imagine, according to his power that is at work
within us, to him be glory...for ever and ever! Amen.

EPHESIANS 3:20–21 NIV

All of God's promises have been fulfilled in Christ
with a resounding "Yes!"

2 CORINTHIANS 1:20 NLT

Jesus Christ is the same yesterday and today and forever.

HEBREWS 13:8 NASB

These things I have written to you who believe in the
name of the Son of God, that you may know that you have
eternal life, and that you may continue to believe in the
name of the Son of God.

1 JOHN 5:13 NKJV

God, we believe that you are who you say you are. Jesus, in you is the fulfillment of God's promise for salvation. Thank you for being faithful to your Word. In you we place our hope. Do more than we can even think to imagine or ask for with our lives. Help us to believe that you will come through even when it's hard for us to see a silver lining in the cloud of circumstance. You are better than our best day together and more faithful than the rising sun.

How does believing God's promises cause you to feel reassured?

Beauty

You are altogether beautiful, my darling,
beautiful in every way.

<small>SONG OF SONGS 4:7 NLT</small>

Your beauty should come from within you—
the beauty of a gentle and quiet spirit that will never
be destroyed and is very precious to God.

<small>1 PETER 3:4 NCV</small>

She puts on strength and honor
as if they were her clothes.
She can laugh at the days that are coming.

<small>PROVERBS 31:25 NIRV</small>

I praise you because you made me
in an amazing and wonderful way.
What you have done is wonderful. I know this very well.

<small>PSALM 139:14 NCV</small>

Lord, when we look at the abundance of diversity in the world around us, we remember that beauty comes in many forms. When you created each of us, you did it intentionally. Thank you that you made us unique on purpose and that beauty is so much more than skin-deep. Let beauty first grow in our hearts, spilling out into the rest of our being. Thank you that we can see the beauty you have placed in each of us when we look for it. We praise you for we are fearfully and wonderfully made.

How do you see God's beauty reflected in each other?

Belief

He must have a strong belief in the trustworthy message he was taught; then he will be able to encourage others with wholesome teaching and show those who oppose it where they are wrong.

TITUS 1:9 NLT

Believe on the Lord Jesus Christ, and you will be saved, you and your household.

ACTS 16:31 NKJV

"All things are possible to him who believes…"

MARK 9:23 NASB

"Have you believed because you have seen me? Blessed are those who have not seen and yet have believed."

JOHN 20:29 ESV

Jesus, we believe that you are the Son of God. You came to earth as a human so we could know what the Father is really like. Above all, you taught us what it means to love without condition. We believe who you were and still are, and we can trust you with our lives and our futures. Thank you for the gift of knowing you. We pray that our belief would lead us into greater confidence in our relationship with you. Thank you that you are near and not distant. Whatever happens in the world around us, we believe that you remain constant.

How can you help each other strengthen your belief in God?

Blessings

Surely, Lord, you bless those who do what is right.
Like a shield, your loving care keeps them safe.

Psalm 5:12 NIRV

Surely you have granted him unending blessings
and made him glad with the joy of your presence.

Psalm 21:6 NIV

Give praise to the God and Father of our Lord Jesus
Christ. He has blessed us with every spiritual blessing.
Those blessings come from the heavenly world. They
belong to us because we belong to Christ. God chose us to
belong to Christ before the world was created. He chose
us to be holy and without blame in his eyes. He loved us.

Ephesians 1:3-4 NIRV

Lord, when we take time to recognize what we have to be thankful for, we realize that your goodness is all around us. When we are feeling overwhelmed, we can practice counting our blessings. The biggest blessing we have is your presence. May the joy of your presence awaken us to life and to your goodness in and around us. We know that you are the giver of all good gifts; today we will be on the lookout for them, knowing that nothing is too big or too small for you.

Which of God's blessings can you thank him for together today?

Boldness

He proclaimed the kingdom of God
and taught about the Lord Jesus Christ—
with all boldness and without hindrance!

ACTS 28:31 NIV

Sinners run away even when no one is chasing them.
But those who do what is right are as bold as lions.

PROVERBS 28:1 NIRV

On the day I called you, you answered me.
You made me strong and brave.

PSALM 138:3 NCV

Let us come boldly to the throne of our gracious God.
There we will receive his mercy, and we will find grace
to help us when we need it most.

HEBREWS 4:16 NLT

Lord, if we have any strength, we know it comes from you. Let us walk boldly into the situations we face, confident that you are with us. With you, there is no need to be timid. We can be courageous in life because we know we can be bold with you. It is in your presence that we are met with the mercy and tenderness of a good father. It is where we receive everything we need. When we are feeling frozen, stuck, or timid, would you remind us of who you are and who we are in you? You have always been faithful to call us into our best selves. We want to be like you, both bold and tenderhearted. Help us to remember that courage does not require perfection, only willingness.

How do you find courage to be both bold and tenderhearted?

Change

Look! I tell you this secret:
We will not all sleep in death,
but we will all be changed.

1 CORINTHIANS 15:51 NCV

He will take our weak mortal bodies and change them
into glorious bodies like his own, using the same power
with which he will bring everything under his control.

PHILIPPIANS 3:21 NLT

Jesus Christ is the same yesterday and today and forever.

HEBREWS 13:8 NIRV

Lord, when change threatens to overwhelm us, help us to remember that change brings with it hope for better things ahead. When it feels as if the bottom has dropped out of life and we don't know what our futures will look like, we know that we can trust in you. You stay the same forever, and there are no mysteries to you. You see and know every step of our journey. You know the end from the beginning and you are not surprised by anything. We trust in you, the unchanging one.

How do you handle change together?

Comfort

God's dwelling place is now among the people, and he will
dwell with them…. "He will wipe every tear from their
eyes. There will be no more death" or mourning or crying
or pain, for the old order of things has passed away.

REVELATION 21:3–4 NIV

May our Lord Jesus Christ himself and God our Father,
who loved us and by his grace gave us eternal comfort
and a wonderful hope, comfort you and strengthen you.

2 THESSALONIANS 2:16–17 NLT

Unless the LORD had helped me,
I would soon have settled in the silence of the grave.
I cried out, "I am slipping!"
but your unfailing love, O LORD, supported me.
When doubts filled my mind,
your comfort gave me renewed hope and cheer.

PSALM 94:17–19 NLT

God, our God, we cannot face our sadness without you. We would be swept away without the light of your love beckoning us to shore. When we are in the throes of grief and sorrow, you are the only peace we know. Help. When we can only mutter that word, rush in with the comfort of your presence, covering us in your overwhelming love. Let the peace that passes understanding spread through us like the warmth of the sun. When we grieve, we know that you are with us; though it may be an end, it is not the end. Breathe hope into our lives again when we need it the most.

Do you feel the comforting presence of God today?

Compassion

When I am with those who are weak, I share their
weakness, for I want to bring the weak to Christ.
Yes, I try to find common ground with everyone,
doing everything I can to save some.

1 CORINTHIANS 9:22 NLT

God, have mercy on me according to your faithful love.
Because your love is so tender and kind,
wipe out my lawless acts.

PSALM 51:1 NIRV

Praise be to the God and Father of our Lord Jesus Christ,
the Father of compassion and the God of all comfort.

2 CORINTHIANS 1:3 NIV

Father of compassion, you are the source of all comfort. You are so kind and patient toward us. Even when we have what feels like nothing to offer, you so willingly draw near with your unfailing love. In our weakness, you don't turn away from us. In the same way, help us not to run away from the weakness we see in others; we want to be like you, lavishly loving those who have nothing to offer us. Thank you for loving better than anyone we've ever known or can imagine. We want to love like you.

How can you be more compassionate with those around you?

Confidence

I can do everything through Christ,
who gives me strength.

PHILIPPIANS 4:13 NLT

Be my rock of refuge,
to which I can always go;
give the command to save me,
for you are my rock and my fortress....
For You have been my hope, Sovereign LORD,
my confidence since my youth.

PSALM 71:3, 5 NIV

Do not throw away your confidence,
which has a great reward.

HEBREWS 10:35 NCV

Lord, when we have nothing to stand on except your Word,
be our strength. When we don't know what to do or where
to turn, we turn to you. You have not failed us yet, and we
believe that you will be with us faithfully every step of our
journey. Thank you that our confidence is not meant to be
found in ourselves—what a relief! We come to you again
today. Be our rock of refuge and our fortress, a safe place
where we find rest from the storms of life.

How do you find your confidence
in God as a couple?

Contentment

To enjoy your work and to accept your lot in life—
that is indeed a gift from God. The person who does that
will not need to look back with sorrow on his past,
for God gives him joy.

ECCLESIASTES 5:20 TLB

I know what it is to be in need, and I know what it is to
have plenty. I have learned the secret of being content
in any and every situation, whether well fed or hungry,
whether living in plenty or in want. I can do all this
through him who gives me strength.

PHILIPPIANS 4:12-13 NIV

Lord, help us to look at our lives and see the gifts within them. Give us eyes to see the beauty of the people you have surrounded us with and the honor it is to serve and love them. Your Word makes it clear that contentment has less to do with what we have and more to do with how we see it. May our minds be trained to see with the lens of plenty, not through the aperture of lack. As we practice the gratitude of what is, rather than what could be, may your joy fill us like a fountain.

How can you choose to be content with life as it is right now?

Delight

When I received your words, I ate them.
They filled me with joy. My heart took delight in them.
Lord God who rules over all, I belong to you.

JEREMIAH 15:16 NIRV

"My God, I want to do what you want.
Your teachings are in my heart."

PSALM 40:8 NCV

Your laws are my treasure;
they are my heart's delight.

PSALM 119:111 NLT

"Let your light shine before others, that they may see
your good deeds and glorify your Father in heaven."

MATTHEW 5:16 NIV

God, giver of all joy, we sometimes forget how happy you are.
You say that you delight in your children—you delight in us!
What a mind-blowing reality. Let your revelation shine in our
minds like the rising sun, bringing light to areas that have
been hidden in darkness. Your joy over us being yours fills our
hearts with incredible wonder. How could we do anything but
be delighted by you? Thank you for your love that surprises
us in the best of ways. You are amazing in your unwavering
opinion of us. Help us to have the same unchanging opinion
of each other, so we continue to believe the best.

How can you help each other realize God's incredible delight?

Depression

The LORD hears his people when they call to him for help.
He rescues them from all their troubles.

PSALM 34:17 NLT

Why am I so sad? Why am I so upset?
I should put my hope in God
and keep praising him.

PSALM 42:11 NCV

You, O LORD, are a shield about me, my glory,
and the lifter of my head.

PSALM 3:3 ESV

He has delivered us from the power of darkness and
conveyed us into the kingdom of the Son of His love.

COLOSSIANS 1:13 NKJV

Faithful Father, we need you to be the lifter of our heads. When darkness clouds our mind and settles over us like an unwelcome haze, we know we cannot wish it away. You, God, are our deliverer. We will choose to put our hope in you no matter what we're feeling. Please do the heavy lifting here. As we choose you, do what only you can do. Let the light of your love shine through the fog of despair and loneliness, bringing relief and freedom. You are our only hope.

Can you sense God's comfort and joy in the middle of your sadness?

Encouragement

The Lord your God is with you;
the mighty One will save you.
He will rejoice over you. You will rest in his love;
he will sing and be joyful about you.

ZEPHANIAH 3:17 NCV

Encourage one another daily,
as long as it is called "Today."

HEBREWS 3:13 NIV

Kind words are like honey—
sweet to the soul and healthy for the body.

PROVERBS 16:24 NLT

Be joyful. Grow to maturity. Encourage each other.
Live in harmony and peace.
Then the God of love and peace will be with you.

2 CORINTHIANS 13:11 NLT

Lord, thank you that we were made for relationship. Would you speak your words over us, bringing life to our whole beings? God of love and peace, may our words be filled with kindness, dripping with grace. When we are feeling down and we encourage others, we will be encouraged ourselves. Let us be those who call out the treasure we see in those around us. As you do the same, our hearts will be strengthened, and our souls will breathe deeply of your love.

How can you encourage each other today?

Eternity

We are citizens of heaven, where the Lord Jesus Christ
lives. And we are eagerly waiting for him to return
as our Savior.

PHILIPPIANS 3:20 NLT

"And if I go and prepare a place for you, I will come back
and take you to be with me that you also may be where I am."

JOHN 14:3 NIV

That will happen in a flash, as quickly as you can wink an
eye. It will happen at the blast of the last trumpet. Then the
dead will be raised to live forever. And we will be changed.

1 CORINTHIANS 15:52 NIRV

Surely your goodness and love will be with me all my life,
and I will live in the house of the Lord forever.

PSALM 23:6 NCV

Lord, thank you that this life isn't all there is. When we have hard days, help us to remember that the taste of your goodness and love we experience here on earth are glimpses of a greater reality. When we dwell in eternity with you, there will be no more sin. There will be no more fear, and there will be no more injustice. Thank you that what we have to look forward to is greater than anything we've known. Remind us that the best is yet to come when we start to forget. We will trust you.

Can you view eternity with a hopeful, happy heart, fully trusting in a good God?

Faithfulness

Your lovingkindness, O LORD, extends to the heavens,
Your faithfulness reaches to the skies.

PSALM 36:5 NASB

The Lord is faithful,
who will establish you and guard you from the evil one.

2 THESSALONIANS 3:3 NKJV

LORD, you are my God; I will exalt you and praise
your name, for in perfect faithfulness you have done
wonderful things, things planned long ago.

ISAIAH 25:1 NIV

The word of the LORD is upright,
and all his work is done in faithfulness.

PSALM 33:4 ESV

Faithful Father, we cannot forget how you have been with us. When we start to question whether you are here now, we look back on our history with you and we see it—we see your faithfulness. You don't change your mind about things or people, and you haven't changed your mind about wanting us as your own. As your children, we cling to you in our weakness. We trust you to do what only you can do. Finish the work you have started and make our paths straight.

How have you seen the faithfulness of God played out in your lives?

Fear

God gave us his Spirit. And the Spirit doesn't make us
weak and fearful. Instead, the Spirit gives us power and
love. He helps us control ourselves.

2 Timothy 1:7 NIRV

The Lord is my light and my salvation—
whom shall I fear?
The Lord is the stronghold of my life—
of whom shall I be afraid?

Psalm 27:1 NIV

When I am afraid, I will trust you.
I praise God for his word.
I trust God, so I am not afraid.
What can human beings do to me?

Psalm 56:3-4 NCV

*Lord of our lives, you are our helper. You are our safe place
and our salvation. We come to you with our fear, knowing
that in your presence, you bring peace and rest. Your Spirit
gives us power when we feel helpless. Thank you that we never
need to stay in a place of worry or despair. When we come to
you, let us hear your perfect truth about our lives and your
good intentions for us. Fear cannot remain when your perfect
love comes in. Thank you for the power of your love.*

What fears can you give to God together?

Forgiveness

"If you forgive other people when they sin against you,
your heavenly Father will also forgive you."

MATTHEW 6:14 NIV

Put up with each other. Forgive one another if you
are holding something against someone.
Forgive, just as the Lord forgave you.

COLOSSIANS 3:13 NIRV

He is so rich in kindness and grace that he purchased our
freedom with the blood of his Son and forgave our sins.

EPHESIANS 1:7 NLT

Sinless, perfect Lord, you've forgiven every wrong we've ever committed. With a heart so open to forgiveness, how it must grieve you when we hold onto a grudge or nurse our anger with each other. Will you help us to extend grace and forgiveness to each other even when we haven't asked for it specifically? Help us to forgive freely and fully, that we may also receive your forgiveness.

Do you need to extend forgiveness to each other today?

Freedom

The Lord is the Spirit,
and where the Spirit of the Lord is, there is freedom.

2 CORINTHIANS 3:17 NIV

My brothers and sisters, you were chosen to be free. But
don't use your freedom as an excuse to live under the
power of sin. Instead, serve one another in love.

GALATIANS 5:13 NIRV

"So if the Son sets you free, you are truly free."

JOHN 8:36 NLT

We have freedom now, because Christ made us free.
So stand strong. Do not change and go back
into the slavery of the law.

GALATIANS 5:1 NCV

Jesus, we know that you came to set the captives free. That means whatever areas we are feeling bound by—sin, fear, or sickness—you have already overcome. When we are feeling stuck, we remember that you chose us to be free. Overwhelm our circumstances with the power of your resurrection, setting us free from any chains. Your ways are so much better than our own, and you move in purpose and power. We invite you into our days; come and set our feet free to dance upon worry, disappointment, and despair. You are greater.

How does it feel to be free from your sin?

Friendship

A friend loves you all the time,
and a brother helps in time of trouble.

PROVERBS 17:17 NCV

There are "friends" who destroy each other,
but a real friend sticks closer than a brother.

PROVERBS 18:24 NLT

"Greater love has no one than this: to lay down one's
life for one's friends. You are my friends if you do what
I command…. Instead, I have called you friends, for
everything that I learned from my Father I have made
known to you."

JOHN 15:13-15 NIV

"In everything, do to others
what you would want them to do to you."

MATTHEW 7:12 NIRV

Jesus, you are the best friend we could ever have. No one knows us the way you do. And yet, you have surrounded us with people who know and love us. Help us, when we are feeling isolated and alone, to reach out to you and to the people we love and trust. We also want to be friends that lay down our own preferences for the good of those we love. Thank you that you created us to be in relationship, not to live alone. Today, as we connect with others around us and with each other, may it draw us closer to you.

What friends spur you on in your relationship with God?

Generosity

Give generously to them and do so without a grudging
heart; then because of this the LORD your God will bless you
in all your work and in everything you put your hand to.

DEUTERONOMY 15:10 NIV

Each of you should give what you have decided in your
heart to give. You shouldn't give if you don't want to.
You shouldn't give because you are forced to.
God loves a cheerful giver.

2 CORINTHIANS 9:7 NIRV

If you help the poor,
you are lending to the Lord—
and he will repay you!

PROVERBS 19:17 NLT

You are so generous, Lord. When we give generously, your blessing pours back on us. Not only does your joy fill our hearts but you replace what we give away. Though we know this to be true, we confess we don't always want to give. Don't let those selfish impulses win. Move us to share all that we have, not only with each other, but with others as well. We have more than we can hold anyway.

How do you feel when you share with others?

Gentleness

"Accept my teachings and learn from me,
because I am gentle and humble in spirit,
and you will find rest for your lives."

MATTHEW 11:29 NCV

"Blessed are those who are humble.
They will be given the earth."

MATTHEW 5:5 NIRV

A gentle answer turns away wrath,
but a harsh word stirs up anger.

PROVERBS 15:1 NIV

Some people have gone astray without knowing it.
He is able to deal gently with them.
He can do that because he himself is weak.

HEBREWS 5:2 NIRV

Gentle Father, your patience and tenderness are so much more than we can fathom. We want to be gentle with our words and actions toward each other and others. Fill us with gentleness that defies our circumstances, so we can reflect your loving attitude no matter what comes our way.

What are some steps you can take to become more gentle with each other?

Goodness

Everything God created is good, and nothing is to be
rejected if it is received with thanksgiving.

1 TIMOTHY 4:4 NIV

Taste and see that the LORD is good.
Oh, the joys of those who take refuge in him!

PSALM 34:8 NLT

My brothers and sisters, I am sure that you are full of
goodness. I know that you have all the knowledge you
need and that you are able to teach each other.

ROMANS 15:14 NCV

Lord, your goodness knows no end. Even when it feels like chaos threatens to drown out the truth of this, we will force ourselves to remember that all good things come from you. Help us to seek out the goodness in our lives—nothing is too small to celebrate. We look for your goodness like children looking for treasure in the world around them. Thank you that when we look for it, we will find it.

Where do you see the goodness of God most in your lives?

Grace

From his fullness we have all received, grace upon grace.

God gives us even more grace,
as the Scripture says,
"God is against the proud,
but he gives grace to the humble."

JAMES 4:6 NCV

Sin is no longer your master,
for you no longer live under the requirements of the law.
Instead, you live under the freedom of God's grace.

ROMANS 6:14 NLT

God, your grace speaks of your kindness. You offer it in abundance to all, especially to those needing it the most. Thank you that your unmerited favor is freely given, and we don't have to prove that we deserve it. Today we remember that your grace has nothing to do with whether or not we do enough. We are so thankful that it has nothing to do with us. We receive your grace in this moment, knowing that it is never like stale bread. You give what is good and right and needed at the right time, and even more than we can ask.

What does God's grace look like in your lives?

Gratitude

I have not stopped giving thanks for you,
remembering you in my prayers.

EPHESIANS 1:16 NIV

Giving thanks is a sacrifice that truly honors me.
If you keep to my path,
I will reveal to you the salvation of God.

PSALM 50:23 NLT

Rejoice always, pray continually,
give thanks in all circumstances;
for this is God's will for you in Christ Jesus.

1 THESSALONIANS 5:16–18 NIV

Give thanks as you enter the gates of his temple.
Give praise as you enter its courtyards.
Give thanks to him and praise his name.

PSALM 100:4 NIRV

God our Father, thank you for your lovingkindness toward us.
Thank you for the gift of family and friends. Thank you that
you have been faithful all our lives. When we are struggling
to see any good, all it takes is stepping back and finding
the small, true things to see those glimpses of grace. We will
practice gratitude until it is as natural as breathing. Thank
you for this very moment we are in. Thank you for perspective.
Thank you for the warmth of the sunshine. Thank you.

What can you thank God for together right now?

Grief

Those who sow in tears shall reap with shouts of joy.

PSALM 126:5 ESV

Let your steadfast love become my comfort
according to your promise to your servant.

PSALM 119:76 NRSV

"Come to me, all you who are weary and burdened,
and I will give you rest.
Take my yoke upon you and learn from me,
for I am gentle and humble in heart,
and you will find rest for your souls."

MATTHEW 11:28-29 NIV

Every valley shall be raised up,
every mountain and hill made low;
the rough ground shall become level,
the rugged places a plain.

ISAIAH 40:4 NIV

All-knowing One, we come to you with burdens weighing us down. Grief has ripped our hearts to shreds. You say that you give rest. Oh, how we need that right now. When we are overcome by sadness at the loss of what could have been, surround us with your comfort and your presence of peace. When we can't even reach out to you, lift us up. You're all we have and the only one who truly knows the depths of what we're walking through. Let your love surround us and bring hope.

Can you ask God for help when you need his comfort?

Guidance

Guide me in your truth and teach me,
for you are God my Savior,
and my hope is in you all day long.

PSALM 25:5 NIV

Wise people can also listen and learn;
even they can find good advice in these words.

PROVERBS 1:5 NCV

We can make our plans,
but the LORD determines our steps.

PROVERBS 16:9 NLT

Those who are led by the Spirit of God
are children of God.

ROMANS 8:14 NIRV

Good Father, we trust that you are leading our steps. You know how much we depend on your guidance. All of our hopes are in you. Even when our plans crumble and there is a detour in the path, we trust that you have better plans than we do. You see the full picture; there are no mysteries to you. We trust that your ways are higher than ours, and your plans are better than those we pursue for ourselves. We yield to your leadership in our lives and shrug off the worries of the unknown. You are a good and faithful leader.

Is there anything God can help guide you in today?

Guilt

God is faithful and fair. If we confess our sins, he will
forgive our sins. He will forgive every wrong thing we
have done. He will make us pure.

1 JOHN 1:9 NIRV

The LORD and King helps me. He won't let me be
dishonored. So I've made up my mind to keep on serving
him. I know he won't let me be put to shame.

ISAIAH 50:7 NIRV

Those who go to him for help are happy,
and they are never disgraced.

PSALM 34:5 NCV

I have not achieved it, but I focus on this one thing:
Forgetting the past and looking forward
to what lies ahead.

PHILIPPIANS 3:13 NLT

Loving God, forgiver of our sins, may the purpose of guilt be that it leads us to reconciliation with you and others. We don't want to be stuck in a cycle of guilt and shame that does nothing but punish us. You are the one who set us free, so we will be free! You have made us clean already. We are not too proud to say when we have messed up. Thank you that we don't need to live in the torment of could haves and should haves. We look to you, the author and finisher of our faith, to lead us into the fullness of forgiveness.

Why doesn't God want us to feel guilt and shame?

Health

The world and its desires pass away,
but whoever does the will of God lives forever.

1 JOHN 2:17 NIV

Don't be wise in your own eyes.
Have respect for the Lord and avoid evil.
That will bring health to your body.
It will make your bones strong.

PROVERBS 3:7-8 NIRV

I will never forget your commandments,
for by them you give me life.

PSALM 119:93 NLT

A happy heart is like good medicine,
but a broken spirit drains your strength.

PROVERBS 17:22 NCV

Lord, we know that you care about every part of our lives. You are not just concerned with our souls, but you also care about every part of our being. Our mind and body are as important to you as our hearts. We trust that you are our healer. Would you touch us today with your healing power, driving every sickness out, healing every broken part? Thank you for knowing us inside out. We pray that your kingdom would come on earth as it is in heaven—in our bodies. We are desperate for your help.

What healing are you believing God for together?

Honesty

Keep me from deceitful ways;
be gracious to me and teach me your law.
I have chosen the way of faithfulness;
I have set my heart on your laws.

PSALM 119:29-30 NIV

"Everything that is hidden will become clear,
and every secret thing will be made known."

LUKE 8:17 NCV

The king is pleased with words from righteous lips;
he loves those who speak honestly.

PROVERBS 16:13 NLT

We will speak the truth in love. So we will grow up in
every way to become the body of Christ.
Christ is the head of the body.

EPHESIANS 4:15 NIRV

God, there is no deceit in you. You never try to trick or mislead us, and your only true enemy is called the father of lies. We hate lies, yet we struggle with lying at times. Forgive our lies and make us brave enough to tell the truth. Even when it might hurt, remind us that lies hurt worse. Help us to be honest with each other so we continue to build a solid foundation of trust in our relationship.

Is there anything you need to be honest about now?

Hope

The LORD is good to those whose hope is in him,
to the one who seeks him.

LAMENTATIONS 3:25 NIV

Hope will never bring us shame.
That's because God's love has poured into our hearts.
This happened through the Holy Spirit,
who has been given to us.

ROMANS 5:5 NIRV

The LORD's delight is in those who fear him,
those who put their hope in his unfailing love.

PSALM 147:11 NLT

God our hope, you are the one we look to today. Meet us in this moment, breathing life into our weary hearts. Fill our minds with your peace. When our path gets bumpy and we are uncertain at how things will turn out, we turn to you. We don't have to know how everything will play out—we just need to know you. We need to know who you are. In you we find our hope. Come close, Lord, and lift our heads. Your unfailing love surrounds us.

Knowing that God always hears you, what can you be hopeful for?

Humility

"Didn't I make everything by my power? That is how all things were created," announces the Lord. "The people I value are not proud. They are sorry for the wrong things they have done. They have great respect for what I say."

ISAIAH 66:2 NIRV

Humble yourselves before the Lord,
and he will lift you up.

JAMES 4:10 NIV

Pride will ruin people,
but those who are humble will be honored.

PROVERBS 29:23 NCV

The LORD has told you what is good,
and this is what he requires of you:
to do what is right, to love mercy,
and to walk humbly with your God.

MICAH 6:8 NLT

Father, your rewards are so generous, and by comparison, your demands are small. You desire humility, and in exchange you promise exaltation. Thank you for reminding us, through your own perfection, how very small we are and how much growing we have to do. Thank you for daily opportunities to earn your rich reward as we recognize our limitations and learn to rely on your greatness. Help us walk in humility with each other daily.

What opportunities have given you a chance to practice humility today?

Identity

See how very much our Father loves us, for he calls us
his children, and that is what we are! But the people who
belong to this world don't recognize that we are God's
children because they don't know him. Dear friends, we
are already God's children, but he has not yet shown us
what we will be like when Christ appears. But we do know
that we will be like him, for we will see him as he really is.

1 JOHN 3:1-2 NLT

Do everything without grumbling or arguing, so that
you may become blameless and pure, "children of God
without fault in a warped and crooked generation." Then
you will shine among them like stars in the sky as you
hold firmly to the word of life.

PHILIPPIANS 2:14-16 NIV

Loving God, thank you that you have called us your children. We get all the benefits of being your kids—that is almost unfathomable! Oh, how we want to be more like you. Thank you that you are changing us into your image even through the hard and dry seasons. When we don't know anything else, we remember that you have called us children. You didn't call us acquaintances, servants, or distant relatives. Father, let our hearts be rooted in this close relationship, knowing that you care for us. Shepherd us and teach us to be like you.

Who do you think God really sees when he looks at you?

Inspiration

The precepts of the LORD are right,
giving joy to the heart.
The commands of the LORD are radiant,
giving light to the eyes.

PSALM 19:8 NIV

Your laws are my treasure;
they are my heart's delight.

PSALM 119:111 NLT

The whole Bible was given to us by inspiration from
God and is useful to teach us what is true and to make us
realize what is wrong in our lives; it straightens us out
and helps us do what is right.

2 TIMOTHY 3:16 TLB

God, you are the Creator of all things. Knowing that we were made in your image means we were also intended to create. When you lift our burdens and bring light to our eyes, there is nowhere we can look that we won't find inspiration. Thank you that you are the source of all inspiring thoughts and ideas. You bring revelation of your kingdom and your ways. You are our delight; we will not forget that. We will remember every good gift you have given, knowing that you are the greatest of them all. Give us eyes to see your creativity and intention in creation today.

How can you find inspiration to create something together?

Intimacy

O Lord, You have searched me and known me.
You know my sitting down and my rising up;
You understand my thought afar off.
You comprehend my path and my lying down,
And are acquainted with all my ways.
For there is not a word on my tongue,
But behold, O Lord, You know it altogether.

Psalm 139:1–4 NKJV

All that I know now is partial and incomplete,
but then I will know everything completely,
just as God now knows me completely.

1 Corinthians 13:12 NLT

God's solid foundation stands firm,
sealed with this inscription:
"The Lord knows those who are his."

2 Timothy 2:19 NIV

God, we long for intimacy with you and each other. What is truly astounding is you long for it with us! You desire us so much that you came to earth and paid for our sins so we could be with you. There is so much you want to share with us, we can only imagine the joy you have when we share what little we have with you. Help us to share with each other vulnerably, knowing that love covers a multitude of sins. Everything we are and have is because of you, so we offer you ourselves today. We love you.

How does being truly known by God and each other encourage you?

Joy

May the God of hope fill you with all joy and peace as you
trust in him, so that you may overflow with hope by the
power of the Holy Spirit.

ROMANS 15:13 NIV

"Don't be sad, because the joy of the Lord
will make you strong."

NEHEMIAH 8:10 NCV

The LORD is my strength and shield.
I trust him with all my heart.
He helps me, and my heart is filled with joy.
I burst out in songs of thanksgiving.

PSALM 28:7 NLT

Always be joyful because you belong to the Lord.
I will say it again. Be joyful!

PHILIPPIANS 4:4 NIRV

God, you say that you give joy to your people. We need to know what it means for your joy to be our strength. Infuse our weary souls today with hope, peace, and relief. We have tasted your joy before, but it almost seems like a distant memory. Would you refresh us with the strength of your love? Rescue us from the troubles that threaten to take us down. Then we will burst into songs of thanksgiving; we will shout for joy, knowing that you have not left us.

What is one truly joyful moment you've shared recently?

Kindness

Be kind to each other, tenderhearted, forgiving one
another, just as God through Christ has forgiven you.

EPHESIANS 4:32 NLT

Kind people do themselves a favor,
but cruel people bring trouble on themselves.

PROVERBS 11:17 NCV

Do you disrespect God's great kindness and favor?
Do you disrespect God when he is patient with you?
Don't you realize that God's kindness is meant
to turn you away from your sins?

ROMANS 2:4 NIRV

Great is his love toward us,
and the faithfulness of the LORD endures forever.
Praise the LORD.

PSALM 117:2 NIV

In your unfailing love, God, we see your kindness. You are so patient. Help us to also be kind in the waiting. Let us be those who forgive quickly, letting go of offense and resentment. We do not want to become hardened shells in these hard times. Help our hearts to stay tender, remembering how much we benefit from your kindness, so we will offer the same to others. Today, we submit our hearts to you again, knowing you are kind and good.

How can you extend kindness to those around you today?

Loneliness

"Teach them to obey everything that I have taught you,
and I will be with you always,
even until the end of this age."

MATTHEW 28:20 NCV

The LORD is near to all who call on him,
yes, to all who call on him in truth.

PSALM 145:18 NLT

Even if my father and mother abandon me,
the LORD will hold me close.

PSALM 27:10 NLT

"Be strong and courageous.
Do not be afraid or terrified because of them,
for the LORD your God goes with you;
he will never leave you nor forsake you."

DEUTERONOMY 31:6 NIV

Lord our God, we need you to meet us right where we are,
in the midst of our loneliness. You said that you will never
leave or forsake us. We need to know the reality of that
in the comfort of your presence. When we feel like no one
understands what we are going through, or would even care
to, you remind us that you never turn away. You are with us
in our mess and failure. You are with us in the mundane and
the ordinary. We will not stop calling on you. You are all we
have. Come through again, Lord, with your peace and life.
Let the closeness of our friendship be the foundation of our
lives and every other relationship.

Can you spend time asking God to surround you with his presence now?

Love

Three things will last forever—faith, hope, and love—
and the greatest of these is love.

1 CORINTHIANS 13:13 NLT

LORD, you are good. You are forgiving.
You are full of love for all who call out to you.

PSALM 86:5 NIRV

Fill us with your love every morning.
Then we will sing and rejoice all our lives.

PSALM 90:14 NCV

Let love and faithfulness never leave you;
bind them around your neck,
write them on the tablet of your heart.

PROVERBS 3:3 NIV

*God, your love is unlike any love we've ever known. We get
to love you because you loved us first. Love is not just an
idea; it is an expression of your very character. Fill us with
your love today. Thank you that it is not conditional; you
never withhold love from those who come to you. Your love is
radical, and we know that if anything can radically change
our hearts, it is that. Let your perfect love drive out every fear
that threatens to keep us captive. May your love be the fuel
that keeps us moving toward you and engaging with those
around us. There is nothing that your love doesn't cover.*

How does the love of God in your life help you love each other and those around you?

Patience

Warn those who are lazy.

Encourage those who are timid.

Take tender care of those who are weak.

Be patient with everyone.

1 THESSALONIANS 5:14 NLT

Be like those who through faith and patience
will receive what God has promised.

HEBREWS 6:12 NCV

Be completely humble and gentle;
be patient, bearing with one another in love.

EPHESIANS 4:2 NIV

Anyone who is patient has great understanding.
But anyone who gets angry quickly
shows how foolish they are.

PROVERBS 14:29 NIRV

God, you know that waiting is hard for us. We know that process is your protocol—most things don't come quickly or easily. We want to be people who have incredible patience and grace for each other and for those around us. When the day at hand feels overwhelming and pointless, help us to see it as part of the bigger picture. Help us to have a broader perspective to know that our decisions and attitudes in the moment have a ripple effect on those around us and on our future. We know that when you meet us in this aspect of our lives, our hearts will change for the better.

How can you show each other more patience?

Peace

"I have told you these things, so that you can have peace
because of me. In this world you will have trouble.
But be encouraged! I have won the battle over the world."

JOHN 16:33 NIRV

The LORD gives his people strength.
The LORD blesses them with peace.

PSALM 29:11 NLT

May the Lord of peace himself give you peace at all times
and in every way. The Lord be with all of you.

2 THESSALONIANS 3:16 NIV

"I am leaving you with a gift—peace of mind and heart.
And the peace I give is a gift the world cannot give.
So don't be troubled or afraid."

JOHN 14:27 NLT

Jesus, you said that in this world we will have trouble, and we know that well. But you also said that you have given us the gift of peace—of mind and heart. No one can take away the peace that you give. We have been full of anxiety and worry which is the opposite of peace. You said it was a gift, so we receive it today with open hands and open hearts. We trust that what you have said you will do.

What does peace look like for you?

Perseverance

In a race all the runners run.
But only one gets the prize.
You know that, don't you?
So run in a way that will get you the prize.

1 CORINTHIANS 9:24-25 NIRV

I have tried hard to find you—
don't let me wander from your commands.

PSALM 119:10 NLT

I have fought the good fight,
I have finished the race,
I have kept the faith.

2 TIMOTHY 4:7 NCV

Let us not become weary in doing good, for at the proper
time we will reap a harvest if we do not give up.

GALATIANS 6:9 NIV

God, when it seems like the only thing we've accomplished is that we haven't totally given up, help us to remember that is a victory. Thank you that this is what perseverance is—holding on. As we continue to walk this life, keep us on the path of light and love. When we start to stray, bring us back. Wherever life may take us, no matter what troubles come or fears rise up, we will cling to you. Remind us, when we get weary, that we are not alone. You have walked this road with us, and you will stay with us until the end. When we don't give up, it's a win. We're counting this moment, this last season of hardship, as that—a win. We're still here, and you're still with us.

What do you feel God calling you to persevere in right now?

Praise

Sing to the LORD a new song,
his praise from the ends of the earth,
you who go down to the sea, and all that is in it,
you islands, and all who live in them.

ISAIAH 42:10 NIV

Praise the LORD from the skies.
Praise him high above the earth.
Praise him, all you angels.
Praise him, all you armies of heaven.
Praise him, sun and moon.
Praise him, all you shining stars.
Praise him, highest heavens
and you waters above the sky.
Let them praise the LORD,
because they were created by his command.

PSALM 148:1-5 NCV

Creator of all things, we know there is always a reason to praise you. Today, we put words to our heart and offer you praise in whatever way is true. Through a song, painting, or poem, we offer you our praise in a new way. You are always worthy, unchanging one. You brought us out of darkness into your wonderful light, and you will do it again. We don't hold back our love from you today. We give you praise because you are our great and high priest whom we can always rely on. You are worthy.

What is something specific you can praise God for together today?

Prayer

LORD, in the morning you hear my voice.
In the morning I pray to you.
I wait for you in hope.

PSALM 5:3 NIRV

Never stop praying.

1 THESSALONIANS 5:17 NIRV

The LORD does not listen to the wicked,
but he hears the prayers of those who do right.

PROVERBS 15:29 NCV

Come, let us bow down in worship,
let us kneel before the LORD our Maker.

PSALM 95:6 NIV

Thank you, Father, that prayer is simply communicating with you. Thank you that you aren't looking for perfect words but for honest and open hearts. When all we can say is, "Help," that is as much a prayer as anything we could script. Today, let this be the beginning of our conversation. We need your help. We need to be in constant communication with you because you are our life source. You are the reason we have life and breath. Hear us as we pray to you today.

What can you pray about right now?

Promises

His divine power has granted to us everything pertaining
to life and godliness, through the true knowledge of Him
who called us by His own glory and excellence.

2 PETER 1:3-4 NASB

Your promises have been thoroughly tested,
and your servant loves them.
My eyes stay open through the watches of the night,
that I may meditate on your promises.

PSALM 119:140, 148 NIV

The LORD always keeps his promises;
he is gracious in all he does.

PSALM 145:13 NLT

If you declare with your mouth, "Jesus is Lord," and
believe in your heart that God raised him from the dead,
you will be saved.

ROMANS 10:9 NIV

All-knowing One, thank you that all your promises will be fulfilled. Even when we've forgotten what you said you would do, you follow through. You are reliable in all you do. Help us to remember when the waiting gets long, unanswered promises are an invitation to persevere; you will do all you have said. When we look at the earth's rhythms and seasons, we remember that winter is not forever; spring is coming. We trust you, giver of all hope.

Which promises of God help you see hope in your current situation?

Protection

My God is my rock. I can run to him for safety.
He is my shield and my saving strength,
my defender and my place of safety.
The LORD saves me from those who want to harm me.

2 SAMUEL 22:3 NCV

The LORD keeps you from all harm
and watches over your life.
The LORD keeps watch over you as you come and go,
both now and forever.

PSALM 121:7–8 NLT

We are pushed hard from all sides. But we are not beaten
down. We are bewildered. But that doesn't make us lose
hope. Others make us suffer. But God does not desert us.
We are knocked down. But we are not knocked out.

2 CORINTHIANS 4:8–9 NIRV

Our protector, we run to you. We cannot do this on our own. Be our defender, our strong tower that shelters us from the wars that are raging. We know that you will care for us; in fact, you have been all along. You do not desert us; no, you don't leave. You are not a memory; you are our living hope. When trouble threatens our very lives, we believe that you are fighting our battles. Tuck us safely in your love, so we can know your peace in that place.

How can you lay down your battle plans and let God be your protector?

Provision

All scripture is inspired by God and is useful for
teaching, for reproof, for correction, and for training in
righteousness, so that everyone who belongs to God may
be proficient, equipped for every good work.

2 TIMOTHY 3:16–17 NRSV

May he give you the power to accomplish all the good
things your faith prompts you to do.

2 THESSALONIANS 1:11 NLT

We are God's handiwork, created in Christ Jesus to do
good works, which God prepared in advance for us to do.

EPHESIANS 2:10 NIV

The LORD reached out his hand and touched my mouth
and said to me,
"I have put my words in your mouth."

JEREMIAH 1:9 NIV

God of our past, present, and future, you know exactly what we need. You never withhold your provision from us. You are a good father who does not give stones when your children ask for bread. We can trust that your goodness covers everything you do, and that every lack we have is met with your abundance. Your Holy Spirit gives us strength where we have none; you fill us with your compassion when we feel our capacity to love is depleted. We cannot give what we do not have. We come to you to be filled with the provision of the fruit of your kingdom—love, joy, and peace. Thank you for all you continually offer us, so we have something to offer each other.

How have you seen God provide for you lately?

Purpose

You have been raised up with Christ.
So think about things that are in heaven.
That is where Christ is.
He is sitting at God's right hand.

COLOSSIANS 3:1 NIRV

We know that in all things God works
for the good of those who love him,
who have been called according to his purpose.

ROMANS 8:28 NIV

My child, pay attention to my words;
listen closely to what I say.
Don't ever forget my words;
keep them always in mind.

PROVERBS 4:20-21 NCV

God, our greatest purpose in life is found in, and flows from, the relationship we have with you. Nothing can compare to who you are. When life spins out of control, and we can't find our feet, we remember that our worth is not in what we do or what we can control. You have chosen us as yours, and you love us unconditionally. We will find our greatest purpose in being who you created us to be in all our uniqueness and in loving each other like it's all that matters.

How do you feel when you think about God having a special purpose for your lives?

Refreshment

The law of the LORD is perfect, refreshing the soul.
The statutes of the LORD are trustworthy,
making wise the simple.

PSALM 19:7 NIV

Jesus replied that people soon became thirsty again after
drinking this water. "But the water I give them," he said,
"becomes a perpetual spring within them, watering them
forever with eternal life."

JOHN 4:13-14 TLB

How priceless is your unfailing love, O God!
People take refuge in the shadow of your wings.
They feast on the abundance of your house;
you give them drink from your river of delights.
For with you is the fountain of life;
in your light we see light.

PSALM 36:7-9 NIV

Generous One, we come to you today, needing your refreshing waters to wash over us. Your Word is living water, satisfying every thirst. Lord, speak your words of life. Awaken our senses with your glorious light. Come to us like rains after a drought, filling every crack and crevice, getting down under the hard crust and refreshing the soil of our hearts. You change everything for the better; we stand under your waterfall of grace, inviting you to wash off everything that hinders us from freedom. Thank you for always being kind and generous. May we be just like you.

In what ways do you feel refreshed by God?

Relationships

Two are better than one,
because they have a good return for their labor:
If either of them falls down,
one can help the other up.

ECCLESIASTES 4:9–10 NIV

Perfume and incense bring joy to the heart,
and the pleasantness of a friend
springs from their heartfelt advice.

PROVERBS 27:9 NIV

Love each other with genuine affection,
and take delight in honoring each other.

ROMANS 12:10 NLT

Gracious God, friend to all, how we thank you for the gift of this relationship. Forgive us for taking it for granted at times. We know how fortunate we are to be blessed with people who love us entirely for who we are. Thank you for the glimpse of your love that close relationships bring. Help us to value and honor our relationship with each other and the many others you have placed in our lives.

What specifically would you like to thank God for in your relationship today?

Reliability

"All people are like grass. All their glory is like the
flowers in the field. The grass dries up. The flowers fall
to the ground. But the word of the Lord lasts forever."

1 Peter 1:24-25 NIRV

Every good action and every perfect gift is from God.
These good gifts come down from the Creator of the sun,
moon, and stars, who does not change like their
shifting shadows.

James 1:17 NCV

You are near, Lord,
and all your commands are true.
Long ago I learned from your statutes
that you established them to last forever.

Psalm 119:151-152 NIV

God, thank you that you are not fickle. You don't make up your mind about something one day and change it the next. Your Word, your every intention, is firmer than the strongest foundations on earth. You do not get caught in a web of lies because you never lie. Thank you that what you say you will do. We trust you to be the same God who carried us through our darkest hours and hard moments. We trust that you are not leaving us to our own devices; no pit of despair will swallow us up. You have been a God who cares, and you will always follow through. We trust you.

How does it make you feel knowing you can rely on God for everything?

Respect

Show respect for all people:
Love the brothers and sisters of God's family,
respect God, honor the king.

1 Peter 2:17 NCV

Trust in your leaders. Put yourselves under their
authority. Do this, because they keep watch over you.
They know they are accountable to God for everything
they do. Do this, so that their work will be a joy. If you
make their work a heavy load, it won't do you any good.

Hebrews 13:17 NIRV

Acknowledge those who work hard among you,
who care for you in the Lord and who admonish you.
Hold them in the highest regard in love
because of their work.
Live in peace with each other.

1 Thessalonians 5:12-13 NIV

God, nothing deserves more respect than you. We know to respect the power of the ocean or the storm, yet we sometimes fail to honor the one who made it, who tells it how far to go. You deserve all our respect, all our love, all our praise. We want to be a couple who respects you and all those you put in authority over us. Help us show respect for each other as well. As we do this, we pray others will learn the same valuable lesson from watching us.

How can you show respect to each other and to God?

Restoration

He has saved us and called us to a holy life—
not because of anything we have done
but because of his own purpose and grace.

2 TIMOTHY 1:9 NIV

Since we have been made right in God's sight by faith,
we have peace with God because of what Jesus Christ our
Lord has done for us. Because of our faith, Christ has
brought us into this place of undeserved privilege where
we now stand, and we confidently and joyfully look
forward to sharing God's glory.

ROMANS 5:1—2 NLT

"Let us praise the Lord, the God of Israel,
because he has come to help his people
and has given them freedom.
He has given us a powerful Savior."

LUKE 1:68-69 NCV

Maker of heaven and earth, you set the stars in motion. You who created all things are the one who also fixes the broken. You see our brokenness: the areas that are filled with unhealthy coping mechanisms, pain, and regret. You are the only hope we have for change. We don't want to repeat the same cycles that perpetuate brokenness. Come and restore all that has been lost. We receive your perfect love, and we welcome your healing power into our deepest pain and insecurity. We trust that the work you started in us, you will complete. Have your way, Lord.

Have you experienced the power of restoration in your life?

Reward

Work willingly at whatever you do, as though you were working for the Lord rather than for people. Remember that the Lord will give you an inheritance as your reward, and that the Master you are serving is Christ.

COLOSSIANS 3:23-24 NLT

"Love your enemies, do good to them, and lend to them without expecting to get anything back. Then your reward will be great, and you will be children of the Most High, because he is kind to the ungrateful and wicked."

LUKE 6:35 NIV

Without faith it is impossible to please God. Those who come to God must believe that he exists. And they must believe that he rewards those who look to him.

HEBREWS 11:6 NIRV

God, help us to remember in every area of life that you are our greatest reward. When we forget what we're living for, bring us back to you. When we're in the throes of sadness and it's hard to see the point of life, remind us that there is a better day coming. When we're in seasons where it feels like all we do is give to others, help us to pour out in love, knowing our reward comes from you. Thank you that you are better than anything we've ever known. We believe that, Lord, even when we don't feel it.

How does it make you feel knowing that God will reward you for your diligence?

Safety

The LORD also will be a refuge for the oppressed,
A refuge in times of trouble.
Those who know Your name will put their trust in You;
For You, LORD, have not forsaken those who seek You.

PSALM 9:9–10 NKJV

The name of the LORD is a strong tower;
The righteous runs into it and is safe.

PROVERBS 18:10 NASB

Wherever I am, though far away at the ends of the earth,
I will cry to you for help. When my heart is faint and
overwhelmed, lead me to the mighty, towering Rock of
safety. For you are my refuge, a high tower where my
enemies can never reach me.

PSALM 61:2-3 TLB

God, when we are vulnerable and afraid, we depend on you to be our keeper. We cry to you for help, and you answer us. Every. Single. Time. We need you to keep us safe; breathe your peace over our minds and hearts when we are tormented by fear. Lead us to your place of rest and recovery where you restore us. Deliver us from our fear and lead us into your love, peace, and joy. We cannot defend ourselves; we rely on you alone.

Do you feel safe when you think about God being near you?

Satisfaction

Because your love is better than life,
my lips will glorify you.
I will praise you as long as I live,
and in your name I will lift up my hands.
I will be fully satisfied as with the richest of foods;
with singing lips my mouth will praise you.

PSALM 63:3–5 NIV

The LORD is all I need.
He takes care of me.
My share in life has been pleasant;
my part has been beautiful.

PSALM 16:5–6 NCV

The poor shall eat and be satisfied; all who see the Lord
shall find him and shall praise his name. Their hearts
shall rejoice with everlasting joy.

PSALM 22:26 TLB

Loving God, you care for all your creation: the flowers of the field and the stars in the heavens. Thank you that you care for us! In a sea of billions, you see us. How could we not be satisfied by who you are? We will pursue your love; we will pursue knowing you and being like you. When disappointments come, they will not break us or shake the confidence that comes from knowing that we are loved. We are completely, wholly, unconditionally loved by you and that is more than enough for us.

Are you satisfied with all God has given you?

Serving

Each of you should use whatever gift you have received to serve others, as faithful stewards of God's grace in its various forms. If anyone serves, they should do so with the strength God provides, so that in all things God may be praised through Jesus Christ.

1 PETER 4:10-11 NIV

Always give yourselves fully to the work of the Lord, because you know that your labor in the Lord is not in vain.

1 CORINTHIANS 15:58 NIV

You were called to freedom…
do not use your freedom as an opportunity for the flesh, but through love serve one another.

GALATIANS 5:13 ESV

God, you are completely worthy of worship, yet you spend all your time thinking of others. Remake us in your image. Devotion to you looks like devotion to others, and we want to give you all our allegiance. Give us a heart that is entirely focused on you and each other. Take away all thoughts of our independence and replace them with expressions of you. We want to serve you and others before we serve ourselves. And we want to do it happily!

How can you serve God and each other today?

Strength

God is our refuge and strength,
an ever-present help in trouble.

PSALM 46:1-3 NIV

The Lord is faithful;
he will strengthen you and guard you from the evil one.

2 THESSALONIANS 3:3 NIRV

Don't be afraid, for I am with you.
Don't be discouraged, for I am your God.
I will strengthen you and help you.
I will hold you up with my victorious right hand.

ISAIAH 41:10 NLT

God, when we have nothing within us to press on, be the strength that keeps us going. You are the one we lean into. Thank you that we don't have to be able to move mountains on our own. We don't have to conjure up the courage to face today in our own strength. We don't know if we could do it if we tried. We need you to be the source of our energy when it feels like we have nothing to give. Thank you that you are faithful in answering us and meeting us right where we are.

In what areas do you need God to be your strength today?

Stress

Praise the LORD, my soul;
all my inmost being, praise his holy name.
Praise the LORD, my soul,
and forget not all his benefits—
who forgives all your sins
and heals all your diseases,
who redeems your life from the pit
and crowns you with love and compassion,
who satisfies your desires with good things
so that your youth is renewed like the eagle's.

PSALM 103:1-5 NIV

Commit your actions to the LORD.
and your plans will succeed.

PROVERBS 16:3 NLT

God, when we are overwhelmed by the worries of life, we come to you. When it seems like we can't keep up with all the demands, we turn to you. When we step back for a moment and invite you in, you bring the clarity we so desperately need. Thank you that your peace is ours in the rush of every day. Would you help us to slow down and let you in, yielding our hearts to you every time we feel overwhelmed? Thank you for being our perfect portion in every circumstance.

When was the last time you were able to let go of stress and just sit with God?

Support

Whom have I in heaven but you?
And earth has nothing I desire besides you.
My flesh and my heart may fail,
but God is the strength of my heart
and my portion forever.

PSALM 73:25–26 NIV

The LORD is near to the brokenhearted
and saves the crushed in spirit.

PSALM 34:18 ESV

You, God, see the trouble of the afflicted;
you consider their grief and take it in hand.
The victims commit themselves to you;
you are the helper of the fatherless.

PSALM 10:14 NIV

*God, you see where we are right now. You know how we need
your support and help. Thank you for being such a faithful
friend; you never leave us to fight our battles alone. We invite
you into every situation where we cannot see a way out
and the ones where we have a plan. We know your ways are
better than ours, and we trust you to turn around the most
impossible situation for your glory and for our good. We love
you, God; we lean on you!*

When do you feel most supported by God?

Sustenance

God is able to bless you abundantly,
so that in all things at all times, having all that you need,
you will abound in every good work.

2 CORINTHIANS 9:8 NIV

I fall to my knees and pray to the Father, the Creator of
everything in heaven and on earth. I pray that from his
glorious, unlimited resources he will empower you with
inner strength through his Spirit. Then Christ will make
his home in your hearts as you trust in him. Your roots
will grow down into God's love and keep you strong.
And may you have the power to understand, as all God's
people should, how wide, how long, how high, and how
deep his love is. May you experience the love of Christ,
though it is too great to understand fully. Then you will
be made complete with all the fullness of life and power
that comes from God.

EPHESIANS 3:14–19 NLT

God, you give us everything we need. Your love is the strength of our lives—the very fuel for our being. In areas where we see a lack right now, we recognize that as an opportunity for your provision. We ask that you would fill us with confidence, courage, and wisdom to recognize what has already been provided to sustain us. You have given us everything we need to live a life that reflects you; help us to see with fresh eyes today all that you have already placed in our lives to this end. You are good!

How do you get your sustenance from God?

Trust

Those who know the LORD trust him,
because he will not leave those who come to him.

PSALM 9:10 NCV

I trust in you, LORD. I say, "You are my God."
My whole life is in your hands.
Save me from the hands of my enemies.
Save me from those who are chasing me.

PSALM 31:14-15 NIV

Yes, the LORD is for me; he will help me.
I will look in triumph at those who hate me.
It is better to take refuge in the LORD
than to trust in people.

PSALM 118:7-8 NLT

God, our God, we have nothing if we don't have you. There is so much confusion in this world—so much in our lives! When we don't understand what is going on and how to navigate it, we will trust you. We trust you to keep leading us even when the path is dark and we don't know where we are headed. We say, like David, that our whole life is in your hands. We are yours and we trust that you will take care of us every step of the way.

How do you know that God is trustworthy?

Truth

"When he, the Spirit of truth, comes,
he will guide you into all the truth."

JOHN 16:13 NIV

The very essence of your words is truth;
all your just regulations will stand forever.

PSALM 119:160 NLT

"If you abide in My word,
you are My disciples indeed.
And you shall know the truth,
and the truth shall make you free."

JOHN 8:31-32 NKJV

Teach me your way, O LORD,
that I may walk in your truth;
unite my heart to fear your name.

PSALM 86:11 ESV

Spirit of truth, you are the freedom-giver to all those who come to you. Your Word is a lamp for our feet, lighting our path. We don't rely on what we think we know; we lean on you to lead us into what is right, true, and just. Your truth stands forever, so let our hearts recognize it clearly. God, when our minds are clouded by confusion, may the truth of your Word be like a beacon in the night. When lies threaten to drown out the whisper of your love, silence them. Thank you that your truth is accessible; you are not too lofty to share your thoughts with us. May the power of your Word cause all other voices to be less distinct than yours.

What steps can you take to incorporate God's truth in your life together?

Understanding

Understanding is like a fountain of life
to those who have it.
But foolish people are punished
for the foolish things they do.

PROVERBS 16:22 NIRV

The teaching of your word gives light,
so even the simple can understand.

PSALM 119:130 NLT

Give me understanding,
so that I may keep your law
and obey it with all my heart.

PSALM 119:34 NIV

Don't act thoughtlessly,
but understand what the Lord wants you to do.

EPHESIANS 5:17 NLT

God, in our confusion, let us not be like fools who lose all understanding. Thank you that the revelation of your Word is simple, reaching us in the most profound, yet ordinary, ways. In our sadness, don't let us lose sight of the simple truths of your gospel. Understanding that life wasn't promised to be easy or pain-free, we can approach you with the questions on our hearts, knowing you will answer us in a way we can comprehend. Thank you for your patience with us.

How do you seek to understand God's will together?

Victory

You can prepare a horse for the day of battle.
But the power to win comes from the LORD.

PROVERBS 21:31 NIRV

Every child of God defeats this evil world,
and we achieve this victory through our faith.

1 JOHN 5:4 NLT

From the LORD comes deliverance.
May your blessing be on your people.

PSALM 3:8 NIV

"The Lord your God is the one who goes with you to fight
for you against your enemies to give you victory."

DEUTERONOMY 20:4 NIV

King of kings, you are the victorious one over all. Every challenger to your power has been, and will be, put in their place. Thank you that today is not the end of our story. Walking through the battlefield of our darkest days, we remember that you said you are coming again. Our hope lies in that day. Thank you that breakthroughs are glimpses of the final victory. We will not give in to despair knowing that you are the winner of every battle.

What was the last victory you experienced together?

Wholeness

He will take our weak mortal bodies and change them
into glorious bodies like his own, using the same power
with which he will bring everything under his control.

PHILIPPIANS 3:21 NLT

Celebrate with praises the God and Father of our Lord
Jesus Christ, who has shown us his extravagant mercy.
For his fountain of mercy has given us a new life—we are
reborn to experience a living, energetic hope through
the resurrection of Jesus Christ from the dead. We are
reborn into a perfect inheritance that can never perish,
never be defiled, and never diminish. It is promised
and preserved forever in the heavenly realm for you!
Through our faith, the mighty power of God constantly
guards us until our full salvation is ready to be revealed
in the last time.

1 PETER 1:3–5 TPT

God of healing, thank you that you do not lead us through this life to be broken beyond repair. In every breaking, there is opportunity for healing and restoration. Though our journey has produced pain and dysfunction, your plans for restoration and wholeness are beautifully weaved through every fiber of our lives. You don't waste a detail. You make the ugliest things beautiful. Thank you for the hope of perfect wholeness to come. What a day that will be!

How does understanding eternal wholeness benefit you in this life?

Wisdom

Wisdom will come into your mind,
and knowledge will be pleasing to you.
Good sense will protect you;
understanding will guard you
It will keep you from the wicked,
from those whose words are bad.

PROVERBS 2:10-12 NCV

Wisdom and money can get you almost anything,
but only wisdom can save your life.

ECCLESIASTES 7:12 NLT

If any of you needs wisdom,
you should ask God for it.
He will give it to you.
God gives freely to everyone
and doesn't find fault.

JAMES 1:5 NIRV

Spirit of wisdom, we rely on you. We need your guidance, with good sense and understanding, to lead us through every decision we make. We know that wisdom is not natural for us. We need you, God, to speak your words of wisdom that bring life and light. Thank you that you are always willing to freely give it, never withholding from those who ask. Today we ask for wisdom in specific areas. We invite your voice to speak to us.

What can you ask for God's wisdom in together today?

Worry

Turn your worries over to the LORD.
He will keep you going.
He will never let godly people be shaken.

PSALM 55:22 NIRV

"Who of you by worrying
can add a single hour to your life?"

LUKE 12:25 NIV

Worry weighs a person down;
an encouraging word cheers a person up.

PROVERBS 12:25 NLT

Do not worry about anything, but pray and ask God for
everything you need, always giving thanks. And God's
peace, which is so great we cannot understand it, will
keep your hearts and minds in Christ Jesus.

PHILIPPIANS 4:6-7 NCV

God, you know how easily worries can overtake our minds. You know how overwhelmed our hearts can get at the thought of everything that could go wrong. We don't want to be weighed down by worry; we give it over to you. We're taking what energy we have and, with thanks, asking for all we need. When worry threatens to shut down our gratefulness and skew our view of life, gently turn us and we will hand it over to you. Thank you for faithfully keeping us going. We trust for your provision in these areas.

What worries can you hand over to God today?

BroadStreet Publishing Group, LLC.
Savage, Minnesota, USA
Broadstreetpublishing.com

Prayers & Promises for Couples

© 2020 by BroadStreet Publishing®

978-1-4245-6011-0 (faux leather)
978-1-4245-6012-7 (ebook)

Design by Chris Garborg | garborgdesign.com
Compiled and edited by Michelle Winger | literallyprecise.com

Printed in China.

20 21 22 23 24 25 7 6 5 4 3 2 1